SCHOLASTIC

Quick Cloze Passages

for Boosting Comprehension

Grades 2–3

Edited by Karen Baicker

NEW YORK • TORONTO • LONDON • AUCKLAND • SYDNEY
MEXICO CITY • NEW DELHI • HONG KONG • BUENOS AIRES

Teaching *Resources*

"The Button Story" from *Reading Passages That Build Comprehension: Context Clues* by Linda Ward Beech.
Copyright © 2005 by Linda Ward Beech. Published by Scholastic Inc. Used by permission of the publisher.

Cover design by Jason Robinson
Interior design by Kathy Massaro
Interior illustration by Mike Gordon

ISBN 978-0-545-30108-4

Text copyright © 2012 by Scholastic Inc.
Illustrations copyright © 2012 by Scholastic Inc.
Published by Scholastic Inc.
All rights reserved.
Printed in the U.S.A.

9 10   40   19 18 17 16 15

Contents

The Passages

Introduction

Welcome to *Quick Cloze Passages for Boosting Comprehension: Grades 2–3*. The cloze-format reading passages in this book are designed to help you teach and reinforce vocabulary and build key reading comprehension and critical thinking skills. Each engaging, fill-in-the-blank passage offers students opportunities to fill in missing words from a companion word list. Because students must interact with the text to fill in the missing words, they become active participants in the reading process.

About the Cloze Passages

- Each passage appears on a single page, so that it is easy to reproduce and distribute. The passages progress from lower to higher reading levels. On page 6, you'll find a listing of Flesch-Kincaid readability levels for each. Use these grade level scores to match the passages to different students' abilities.

- The high-interest passages comprise both fiction and nonfiction. They have also been selected to support the following content area topics: history, science and technology, geography, arts and entertainment, and sports and games.

- Each word list includes all of the word choices students need to complete the passage, helping them identify vocabulary that might otherwise be beyond their reach. The target words, like the passages, progress from easier to more challenging. These words have been chosen to build reading skills and stretch students' vocabulary with words they are likely to encounter in other contexts.

- To determine the right word for each blank, students practice key reading comprehension skills, such as tapping prior knowledge of the topic and using context clues.

- At the end of each passage, a Think About It question gives students practice in building different reading comprehension skills, such as analyzing character, identifying details, summarizing, and making inferences. The chart at the bottom of page 6 shows the skills targeted in the Think About It question for different passages.

Teaching Tips

- Refer to page 7 to see how the activities in this book align with the Common Core State Standards.

- You can use the activities to assess students' progress and to provide preparation for standardized tests. To monitor students' work, see the answer key on page 48.

Introducing the Cloze Passages

Model for students how to work with the cloze passages by having them follow these steps:

1. Read the title, introduction, and then the passage. Get a feel for what it's about and why it was written. Don't try to fill in any words yet.

2. Reread the entire passage. Think about the kind of word that might fit each blank. Look at the other words in the sentence for clues about the word that is missing.

3. Read through the word list. Look for the words that are closest in meaning to the words you're already considering.

4. When you find a match, write it in the blank.

5. When you've completed the passage, read it through with your answers in place to make sure it makes sense.

Ways to Use the Cloze Passages

The cloze passage activities are flexible and easy to use in a variety of ways:

- **Small Group:** Distribute copies of the same passage to each member of a small group (4–5 students). Have students read and fill in the blanks. Then have them trade passages to check each other's work. One student can read the completed passage aloud.

- **Individual Desk Work While Conferencing:** Distribute a passage to each student to work on while you conference with individual students about their cloze passages or about other academic subjects.

- **Homework:** Send copies of passages home for vocabulary reinforcement and reading practice, and for students to complete with their families as a school-home connection.

Do More!

- Distribute the cloze passages without the word list. Let students try to come up with their own vocabulary choices and read their passages aloud to the class.

- Once students have gotten the hang of cloze passages, you can also create your own using other classroom materials, such as picture books, science texts, and social studies passages. Photocopy the passage once and use correction fluid to create blank spaces. Include a word list of the missing words in alphabetical order.

Quick Cloze Passages for Boosting Comprehension: Grades 2–3 © 2012 by Scholastic Teaching Resources

Readability Levels of the Passages

The chart below indicates the Flesch-Kincaid reading level for each of the passages. You can use these grade-level scores to determine which passages are appropriate for the abilities of different students.

1	What's in My Pocket?	RL 1	21	Art From Junk	RL 3.2
2	The Stars and Stripes	RL 1	22	Elbows Off the Table	RL 3.3
3	Stuck!	RL 1.1	23	A Tall Tale	RL 3.3
4	Wild, Wild Snowstorm	RL 1.7	24	The Great Wall of China	RL 3.4
5	What Did You Say?	RL 1.7	25	The Rescue	RL 3.4
6	Cat Chat	RL 1.9	26	Animals of Australia	RL 3.4
7	A Visit From the Sea	RL 2.0	27	Rats in the Classroom	RL 3.7
8	Why the Bear Has a Short Tail	RL 2.0	28	Kid Inventors	RL 3.8
9	My Favorite Dentist	RL 2.1	29	How Leopard Got His Spots	RL 3.9
10	It's Slinky™ Time!	RL 2.1	30	Vanishing Frogs	RL 4.0
11	The Snowflake Boy	RL 2.2	31	The Best Sand Castle	RL 4.1
12	Oh, No!	RL 2.3	32	The Story of Ping Pong	RL 4.2
13	Go, Dog, Go!	RL 2.5	33	America's Lady Liberty	RL 4.5
14	The Button Story	RL 2.6	34	Life in Space	RL 4.6
15	Here Comes the Parade!	RL 2.6	35	Leonardo da Vinci	RL 4.7
16	You Can't Throw It Away	RL 2.7	36	An American Volcano	RL 4.9
17	Home, Sweet Home!	RL 3.0	37	*Titanic*!	RL 5.4
18	Lunch Lady	RL 3.0	38	Jackie Robinson: American Hero	RL 5.5
19	Mystery on the Beach	RL 3.1	39	Three Cheers for Chocolate	RL 5.6
20	Tickled Silly	RL 3.2	40	Vets Behind the Scenes	RL 5.6

Building Comprehension Skills

The chart below shows the reading comprehension skill targeted in the Think About It question for different passages.

Skill	Passage #
Analyze Character	1, 8, 18, 21, 23, 38
Recognize Cause & Effect	7, 34, 36, 37
Compare & Contrast	3, 4, 17, 26, 28, 32
Distinguish Between Fact & Opinion	33, 39

Skill	Passage #
Identify Details	10, 12, 13, 19, 31, 35, 40
Make Inferences	2, 5, 9, 11, 14, 16, 22, 30
Understanding Sequence	20, 25, 29
Summarize	6, 15, 24, 27

Name _____ Date _____

The Stars and Stripes

Read this poem to find out about the stars and stripes on our flag. Use the word list to fill in the blanks.

Word List

history
praise
proudly
salute
special

We live in the land of the free.

Our flag flies high for all to see.

Red, white, and blue are the colors we see.

The flag tells about our country's _____.

The story begins with thirteen stripes,

Seven are red, and six are white.

From one to fifty—now count each star.

That's how many states there are!

We fly the flag on _____ days.

We _____ the flag and give it _____.

Oh, say can you see, in this land of the free,

How _____ our flag flies for you and me?

Think About It!

What are some reasons people fly the U.S. flag?

Stuck!

Was it hard to travel west in a covered wagon? Fill in the blanks as you read about one boy's journey.

June 4, 1864

My parents and I are going west. Each day our scout,

Nat, rides _____ looking for good

trails for our wagon train.

It rained all last night. That turned the paths to mud.

I was driving our wagon when it _____

into a _____. Our wheels got stuck

in that hole! I tried to get them rolling again. All I did was

_____ mud around.

Soon, Nat rode up with a huge ox and a rope. He tied

the ox to the wagon. After one _____ tug,

we were free!

Word List

- **ahead**
- **mighty**
- **rut**
- **slipped**
- **splash**

Think About It!

How was traveling by covered wagon different from traveling by car?

Quick Cloze Passages for Boosting Comprehension: Grades 2–3 © 2012 by Scholastic Teaching Resources

Name _____ Date _____

Wild, Wild Snowstorm

Have you ever seen a blizzard? Fill in the blanks in this article to find out about these wild storms.

A blizzard is a wild snowstorm. It snows for hours and hours. Sometimes, it snows for days! The air is _____ cold. Strong _____ of wind make trees sway and cause high _____. These mounds of snow can bury cars. It might take days, even weeks to _____ the cars.

Whiteouts are caused by _____ snow. That's when the sky and ground look like a big white sheet! It's easy to get lost in a whiteout.

Protect yourself and your pets during a blizzard. Stay inside until the snow stops. Then go out and have some fun!

Word List

freezing
gusts
drifts
swirling
uncover

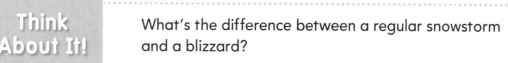

Think About It!

What's the difference between a regular snowstorm and a blizzard?

Name _____ Date _____

What Did You Say?

Can you always believe your ears? Fill in the blanks in this article to find out why you can't.

One day, my friend said to me, "I was on my way to the party. Of course, I was dressed to the nines. Then it started to rain cats and dogs. I got _____! I was fit to be tied!"

Did you understand what she said? If not, it's because she used idioms. Idioms are sayings that have special _____. "Dressed to the nines" means, "looking your best." That makes _____—she was going to a party!

"Raining cats and dogs" is an idiom, too. It doesn't have to do with falling animals! It just means that it's really _____ outside.

And what did my friend mean when she said she was "fit to be tied?" She meant that she was very upset. Well, I can understand why! Her party clothes were probably _____ in that rain. I'd be fit to be tied, too!

Word List

drenched
meanings
pouring
ruined
sense

Think About It!

Why do people use idioms when they speak and write?

Quick Cloze Passages for Boosting Comprehension: Grades 2–3 © 2012 by Scholastic Teaching Resources

Cat Chat

Can cats talk? Fill in the blanks to learn why the author says, "My cat tells me a lot."

My cat, Pearl, can't really talk, but she tells me a lot. She does so in her own way. Pearl certainly knows how to _____ her feelings. I just have to pay _____ to what she does.

Like all cats, Pearl says, "meow." One kind of meow is a friendly _____. It means, "Hello, I'm glad to see you."

A very loud meow is _____. It means, "Look at me! Something is wrong! I need help!"

Pearl's purr sounds like a motor. It tells me very clearly that she is happy. Pearl purrs softly when she smells food and when I pet her.

If Pearl rubs against my leg, I know she's saying, "I'm hungry!" When she rolls on her back and _____, she's saying, "I like you and trust you." My cat tells me a lot.

Word List

attention
communicate
different
greeting
stretches

What are some of the ways Pearl communicates?

Quick Cloze Passages for Boosting Comprehension: Grades 2–3 © 2012 by Scholastic Teaching Resources

Name _____ Date _____

A Visit From the Sea

Through the ages, people have told stories about the sun and the moon. Fill in the blanks as you read one story about how the sun and moon came to live in the sky.

Way back when, the Sun and the Moon were very good friends with the Sea. Every day, Sun and Moon visited Sea. But Sea never visited the Sun and Moon, and that hurt their feelings.

Finally, they asked Sea why he never visited. "Your house is not big enough," said Sea. "I couldn't fit."

So Sun and Moon built a _____ house. It was so big that it took a whole day to walk across it. Surely, Sea would fit.

The next day, Sea visited. He _____ into the house until the water was waist high. "Should I stop?" he asked.

"No, no," said Sun and Moon. So Sea kept flowing. Soon, he reached the _____. Sun and Moon had to sit on the roof.

Finally, the whole house was _____, including the roof. Sun and Moon had to leap onto a cloud _____ by. And that's how Sun and Moon came to live in the sky.

Word List

ceiling
floating
flowed
huge
underwater

Think About It!

What caused Sun and Moon to live in the sky?

Quick Close Passages for Boosting Comprehension: Grades 2–3 © 2012 by Scholastic Teaching Resources

Why the Bear Has a Short Tail

Why do big bears have small tails? Read this folktale to find out. Use the word list to fill in the blanks.

Many winters ago, Bear had a long, _____

tail. Then one day, he spotted Fox carrying a

_____ of fish. "Where did you get all of

those fish?" Bear inquired.

Sly Fox did not like Bear. Fox had also stolen the fish,

and he did not want Bear to know that he had taken them

without _____. So Fox decided to trick Bear.

"I went fishing," Fox replied. "So can you. Go to the lake, cut a hole

in the ice, put your tail in the water, and you will catch a lot of fish!"

Bear went down to the lake, hoping to catch his dinner. He carefully

cut a hole in the ice and _____ his tail.

Soon the water _____ solid. Poor Bear's tail got stuck

in the ice! When Bear pulled hard to get his tail out, part of it snapped off.

Ever since then, all bears have had short tails.

Word List

beautiful
froze
load
lowered
permission

Think About It!

Describe two things Fox did that shows he could not be trusted.

Quick Cloze Passages for Boosting Comprehension: Grades 2–3 © 2012 by Scholastic Teaching Resources

Name _____ Date _____

My Favorite Dentist

**Do you like to go to the dentist? Many kids don't…
but fill in the blanks to read a story about one kid
who does.**

Some kids are scared to go to the dentist, but not

me. I have a funny dentist, named Dr. Smileyface. I

don't think that's his real name, but that's what he tells

the kids. He has a cool _____

room with _____ games and a

big toy box. He asks goofy questions like, "Are you

_____ yet?" and "Do you eat flowers to make your

breath smell sweet?" One time, he told me this joke. "What has lots of

teeth, but never goes to the dentist…? A _____!"

When I laughed, he pulled my tooth. It didn't hurt at all. He also

tells me to brush so I don't get a _____ the

size of the Grand Canyon. When I leave, he sends me home with a

_____. Last time, it was a rubber spider to scare my

mom with. Now she's afraid of my trips to the dentist!

Word List

- cavity
- comb
- married
- surprise
- video
- waiting

Think About It!

Why do you think the dentist does such silly things?

Quick Close Passages for Boosting Comprehension: Grades 2–3 © 2012 by Scholastic Teaching Resources

Name _____ Date _____

It's Slinky™ Time!

Have you ever wondered who made the first "Slinky™"? Read this article to find out. Use the word list to fill in the missing words.

Have you ever played with a Slinky™ toy?

It looks like a snake, but it's made from thin wire or

plastic. Stretch it out, then let it go. It can "walk"

down stairs!

Richard James _____

the Slinky™ toy in 1945. He _____

a gigantic spring fall off a shelf. It rolled over a table and

_____ to the floor. James thought it

could be an _____ toy. It took several

years to get it right. Then, he sold 400 in one day! Next, James

made a _____ to coil the wire. Millions of

Slinky™ toys have been sold since.

Word List

amusing
invented
machine
tumbled
watched

Think About It!

What gave Richard James the idea for the Slinky™?

Name _____ Date _____

The Snowflake Boy

Have you ever really looked at a snowflake?
Fill in the blanks to read about someone who has.

Willie Bentley loved snow. He liked to

_____ the flakes. He tried to draw

them. He tried to hold them. But they would always melt

on his warm hands!

    One day, he got a new _____.

Willie tried and tried to take a good picture. He wanted a

close-up picture of just one snowflake. The pictures were

all too dark.

    He _____ learned how to take good pictures

up close and saw that no snowflakes were alike!

    When he was a grown-up, people called Willie "Snowflake Bentley."

He put all his _____ in a book. At last he could

share the _____ snowflakes.

Word List

camera
finally
photographs
study
wonderful

Think About It!

Why do snowflakes stick to the ground if they don't stick
to Willy's hand?

18

Quick Click Passages for Boosting Comprehension, Grades 2–3 © 2012 by Jeannette Sanderson, Scholastic Teaching Resources

Name _____ Date _____

Oh, No!

How do rumors get started? Fill in the blanks to find out how one rumor was spread.

One day a hare was sleeping _____ a

tree. Then something fell down with a loud THUD! The

ground shook. The hare jumped up and started running. He

shouted, "Oh no! The earth is breaking apart!"

A deer spotted him and asked, "What's the matter?"

"The earth is breaking apart!" said the _____ hare.

The deer followed the hare. They ran past a rhinoceros.

The earth is breaking apart!" they shouted. The rhino joined them.

A lion heard the animals _____ by. "What's the

matter?" he asked. They told him that the earth was breaking apart. "The

earth seems quite _____ to me. Just how did this tale get

started?" the lion asked.

The hare explained, and said, "Follow me."

When they reached the tree, something fell to the earth with a THUD!

The lion _____. "You heard this coconut hitting the

ground. Don't listen to rumors!"

Word List

beneath
laughed
solid
terrified
thundering

Think About It!

Why did the hare think the earth was breaking apart?

Name _____ Date _____

Go, Dog, Go!

Some people play catch with their dogs, or take them for a run. Fill in the blanks to find out about some sports that are just for dogs.

D ogs play sports. Some dogs play catch. Some go swimming.

In Alaska, dogs are famous for _____ in

sled races with their owners. But dogs don't have to play human

sports. Dogs have their very own sports to play.

Dog shows are a _____ of dog sport.

Dogs can win at different kinds of contests. In one contest,

called Dog Agility, dogs run an obstacle course.

An obstacle is something that gets in your way. Dogs must

walk over a swinging bridge. They must _____

around poles. They must jump over fences and crawl through

_____. Dogs are _____

on how well and how quickly they run the course.

Dogs enjoy sports, just as humans do. They like working to become

really good at their sport. They even enjoy _____

for their fans.

Word List

competing
performing
scored
tunnels
type
weave

Think About It!

What does a dog need to do to win a Dog Agility contest?

Name _____ Date _____

The Button Story

Men's jacket sleeves often have buttons on them . . . but they don't button! Read this story to find out one reason why. Fill in the blanks using words from the word list.

Why are there buttons on the sleeves of men's jackets? Some say it is because of Frederick the Great. This king led his men in many wars. He liked the

_____ to look neat. But their sleeves

were always _____. That's because

the soldiers wiped the _____

from their faces on their sleeves. Frederick was

_____ about this. He was so angry that

he had buttons sewn on the _____

sleeves of all his men. It's hard to wipe your face on a button!

Word List

filthy
outraged
sweat
troops
uniform

Think About It!

Why might Frederick the Great care about how his troops looked?

Name _____ Date _____

Here Comes the Parade!

Every Thanksgiving there is a big parade in New York City. Fill in the blanks to find out all about it.

Thanksgiving is a busy day. The night before is busy, too, at least in New York City. Macy's workers pump up _____ balloons! They are for the Macy's Thanksgiving Day Parade. In the morning, people will crowd the streets. _____ will watch it on TV.

There are dozens of balloons. Some of them are ten stories high! They are filled with air. The air is mixed with a gas called _____. This gas makes them float high in the air. _____ walk down the street and hold the balloons down with ropes.

Here's Kermit! There's Buzz Lightyear! Look at Shrek, over there! The big balloons look alive. They look out with their big eyes.

Every year, there are new balloons. Thousands of kids write letters to the _____ who plan the parade. They ask for new balloons. The parade planners try to use their ideas. Maybe you could come up with an idea for next year's parade!

Word List

- directors
- giant
- helium
- millions
- volunteers

Think About It!

What happens at the Macy's Thanksgiving Day Parade?

Quick Case Passages for Building Comprehension, Grade 2 © 2012 by Scholastic Teaching

Name _____ Date _____

You Can't Throw It Away

What keeps coming back no matter how often you throw it away? Fill in the blanks in this article to find out.

Want to play catch by yourself? You can—

with a boomerang. Long ago, hunters in Australia used

boomerangs as _____ for hunting. But

today, they are used for fun. Try throwing one as hard as you

can. If you've done it right, the boomerang circles around

and _____ to you.

The secret is in its shape. Most boomerangs have an

elbow. That gives it a bend in the middle and two "wings." They work

just like _____ wings.

As a boomerang flies through the air, its wings spin. Each wing

turns around the other wing. That makes it fly in a circle. Throwing a

boomerang can be tricky. Hold it close to your body, just above your

_____. Hold the boomerang straight up and down.

Now snap your wrist and throw! With practice, you can release it and

make it come back to _____ the same spot.

Word List

airplane
exactly
returns
shoulder
weapons

Think About It!

How were boomerangs useful during hunting long ago?

Name _____ Date _____

Home, Sweet Home!

How do ants and termites build their homes? Fill in the blanks in this article to find out.

Tiny insects build the most _____ homes. They build them to protect themselves and their families.

Ants build _____ mazes of tunnels and rooms. There are _____ for eggs, places to store food, and rooms for sleeping. They are always working on their homes. New tunnels are built. Walls are _____. The ants work so hard that they need to sleep all winter!

Termites build castles. They make tiny holes on the outside to create an air-conditioning _____!

Some termite mounds are shaped like mushrooms. Others are shaped like barrels. And some are as tall as giraffes.

Termites make mud using dirt and spit. Then they use this mud to build homes with very strong, thick walls. Farmers sometimes have to clear termite nests from their fields. Some towers are so strong that the only way to shatter them is to blow them up with _____!

Word List

amazing
chambers
dynamite
system
underground
repaired

Think About It!

How are ant and termite homes alike? How are they different?

Quick Cloze Passages for Boosting Comprehension: Grades 2–3 © 2012 by Scholastic Teaching Resources

Name _____ Date _____

Lunch Lady

Is there someone at school you admire? Fill in the blanks from the word list as you read about the school worker one girl admires most.

I don't know her name. I just call her "Lunch Lady." There are _____ nice women in the _____, but Lunch Lady is the nicest of all. Every day, she smiles at me when I go through the line. She says things like, "Hi Maggie! Are you having a good day?"

Lunch Lady always _____ that I like chicken strips the best. Whenever that's what is being served, she hands me the strips and says, "Look, your _____!"

One day, I dropped my tray. Food went all over the floor. I was so _____, but Lunch Lady came to my rescue. She helped me clean up the mess, and told me, "Don't worry about it. It's okay!"

Another time, I was at the shoe store with my dad, and I saw Lunch Lady. She gave me a big hug. The reason I admire Lunch Lady is because she's friendly and kind.

Word List

cafeteria
embarrassed
favorite
remembers
several

Think About It!

Name two things the Lunch Lady does that shows she is kind.

Name _____ Date _____

Mystery on the Beach

**The natural world has mysteries that no one can figure out.
Fill in the blanks in this article to find out about one of them.**

One night in Mexico, on a moonlit beach, a baby is
born. In the dark, the baby leaves the beach. She travels
_____ of miles away. Fifty years later,
she returns to the same place where she was born.

   Who is this mysterious female? She is a type of sea turtle.
During the summer months, many swim as far north as Long
Island, New York, to _____ on crabs and other local
_____. But at nesting time, they all head for the same
place—the beach on the gulf coast of Mexico where they were born.

   Then, all at once, the turtles leave the water! They use their
_____ to dig nests in the sand. Then they lay their eggs.

   About eight weeks later, baby turtles _____.
In the moonlight, they too find their way to the sea. Someday, the females
will return to this beach. How will they know when and where to go?
That is the mystery.

Word List

flippers
hatch
munch
seafood
thousands

Think About It!

What is the mystery of the sea turtles?

Quick Cloze Passages for Boosting Comprehension: Grades 2–3 © 2012 by Scholastic Teaching Resources

Name _____ Date _____

Tickled Silly

Why do we laugh when someone tickles us? Fill in the blanks in this article to find out.

Most of us don't like to be tickled. We try to wiggle and _____ away. Yet no matter how much we _____ it, we end up laughing. Why?

Some scientists wanted to find out. First, the team needed to _____. They spent some time tickling each other. Then they gathered a group of students who were willing to be tickled for the good of _____.

Next, they watched students laughing at different TV shows. They wanted to see different types of laughing. They tickled the volunteers in the ribs, under the arms, and on the toes. They even used a tickling machine.

What did they learn? People do not laugh because tickling is funny. Laughing is a reflex. It's something that happens that you can't _____, like sneezing and blinking.

Word List

control
dislike
practice
science
squirm

Think About It!   What did scientists do first to find out about tickling?

Name _____ Date _____

Art From Junk

What did one artist do with a pile of junk? Read this article to find out. Then fill in the blanks using words from the word list.

Alexander Calder's father was a sculptor. His mother was a painter. He became an artist, too.

As a child, Calder loved to save scraps. He collected pieces of string, wire, and cans. Calder used these pieces to make toys and _____.

As an _____, Calder used scraps to make sculptures. Sculptures are statues or figures. They can be made from all kinds of things. Calder used his "junk" to make art.

What kind of art can you _____ out of junk? Calder made a rooster out of cans. He made a tiny dog using a _____ for its head. He made sculptures using metal scraps. Some had parts that moved. They were called _____. Calder was famous for his scrap metal art. Like both his parents, Calder worked hard at making art that others would enjoy.

Word List

adult
clothespin
construct
gadgets
mobiles

Think About It!

What words would you use to describe Calder?

28

Elbows Off the Table!

Why did table manners come about?
Fill in the blanks in this article to find out.

Why do we have rules for eating? The story of knives, forks, and spoons may tell us.

Long ago, people ate with their fingers. They took their food from one large pot. Everyone was _____ to have clean hands before eating.

In 1530, a book of manners for children was written. It said that putting more than three fingers in the pot at once was _____!

Knives were the first silverware. People could _____ pieces of meat that were too hot to pick up.

Only rich people used forks and spoons in the 1700s. By the 1800s, most people could _____ them. People wanted to use the new forks and spoons correctly. They followed _____ rules. The rules warned people never to eat with their fingers. They also said to be quiet and tidy.

Word List

afford
rude
stab
strict
supposed

Think About It!

Why do people use silverware?

Name _____ Date _____

A Tall Tale

Tall tales are funny because everything is exaggerated—bigger and better than real life. Fill in the blanks in this tall tale using words from the word list.

Paul Bunyan was a mighty man. He was so big, he had to use wagon wheels for buttons. Paul was a lumberjack. He owned a blue ox named Babe. Paul and Babe were so big that their _____ made 10,000 lakes in the state of Minnesota.

Word List

drill
mosquitoes
terrible
thawed
tracks

Paul worked with seven axmen. They were so big that they were six feet tall sitting down. All of them were named Elmer. So when Paul called "Elmer!" they all came running.

The year of the two winters, it got so cold that when the axmen would speak, their words froze in midair. When it _____ in the spring, there was a _____ chatter for weeks.

One time, Paul caught two giant _____ and used them to _____ holes in maple trees.

Paul Bunyan had a purple cow named Lucy. In the year of two winters, it got so cold that Lucy's milk turned to ice cream before it hit the pail!

Think About It!

What do these tall tales suggest about Paul Bunyan?

Name _____ Date _____

The Great Wall of China

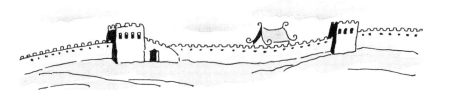

Fill in the blanks in this article to learn about one of the most amazing structures ever built.

What's the biggest wall you've ever seen? Is it 30 feet tall? Is it thousands of miles long? Does it show up in some pictures from space? Probably not. There's only one wall that big. It's the Great Wall of China.

Two thousand years ago, China had many

_____. The emperor thought a strong

wall would keep China _____. He had

people mend old walls. He had them build new walls out of stone

and mud. Then they _____ them all, making

one 3,000-mile-long wall! For the next 1,000 years, other emperors

_____ the wall. Finally, it stretched for 4,500 miles.

Some of it has crumbled. But much of it still stands today.

It is a _____ of national pride.

Word List

connected
enemies
extended
secure
symbol

Think About It! What were the steps taken to build the Great Wall?

Name _____ Date _____

The Rescue

What happens when a cat gets stuck in a tree? Fill in the blanks to find out.

Mia's black cat climbed to the top of a

_____ pole and couldn't come down.

"Come down, Spooky!" cried Mia. Mia thought hard.

What could she do? She went across the street to ask Mr.

Carson for help. He was a firefighter before he retired.

"What's the matter, Mia?" asked Mr. Carson.

"My cat is up on that pole, and I can't get her down!"

Mr. Carson hugged Mia and said, "I'll call my _____

at the fire station. They will come and help."

A few minutes later, Mia saw the fire truck coming. The firefighters

parked near the pole and raised a long ladder to the top. A firefighter

climbed the ladder and reached out for Spooky. Just then, Spooky

_____ to a nearby tree limb, climbed down the tree,

and ran into the _____. Mia said, "Spooky! You

_____ cat!" Mr. Carson and the firefighters laughed

and laughed.

Word List

backyard
buddies
naughty
sprang
telephone

Think About It! What steps were taken to rescue Spooky?

Name _____ Date _____

Animals of Australia

What unusual animals live in Australia? Fill in the blanks in this article to read about them.

Can you find Australia on a world map? It is a very large island. It is also one of the seven _____. Most of its people live near the coast. The middle of Australia is very dry. Some of it is _____. Not too many people live there. But many unusual animals do!

You may recognize Australia's most famous animals. They are kangaroos. They have _____ back legs for hopping. Kangaroos are big, but they can hop very fast. Kangaroo babies are called joeys. Joeys spend their first few months riding in their mother's _____.

You may also know koalas. Some people think they look like teddy bears! But they're not bears at all. Koalas spend almost all of their time in trees. They stay there to avoid bigger animals below.

Now look to the water to find the platypus. Its _____ feet and flat bill make it look like a duck with fur!

Word List

- continents
- desert
- pouches
- powerful
- webbed

Think About It!

What does the platypus have in common with a duck?

Name _____ Date _____

Rats in the Classroom!

Rats in class?! Read this story to learn how a rat is helping schools. Use the word list to fill in the blanks.

EEK! A little white rat just _____

across the floor! Time to run for cover, right? Not if that rat

belongs to Judy Reavis.

    For the past two years, "Rattie" has had a job in

California schools. She connects _____

to the Internet. "I call her my little rat wirer!" Judy says.

    First, Judy wraps a string around Rattie's middle. The string is

attached to an Internet cable. The well-trained rat then does a job no

_____ can do. She _____ behind

walls and goes under floors. She even crawls along ceiling panels to

find the quickest route to her goal.

    Judy waits at the end point with Rattie's favorite treats—cat food

and candy. "Rattie knows how to find the shortest path to her

_____!" Judy explains. When she is done, Judy unties

the string. Then she pulls the Internet cable through the path that Rattie

has just found.

Word List

- classrooms
- darted
- human
- reward
- squeezes

Think About It!

How does the rat help connect computers to the Internet?

Quick Cloze Passages for Boosting Comprehension: Grades 2–3 © 2012 by Scholastic Teaching Resources

Name _____ Date _____

Kid Inventors

What's your favorite toy? How do you think it was first invented? Fill in the blanks to find out what two kids invented.

Toys and games are fun, but inventing them is serious

_____. At big toy companies, there are

adults who do nothing but think up new toys. But some of

the best inventions are made by kids.

Thirteen-year-old Casey Golden loved to play golf.

He invented a way to make the game more "green." He

_____ a new golf tee. It is called the Biotee®.

Most golf tees are made from wood, but Casey's tee is made

out of _____ paper. Casey started his own

_____ to make the new tee. Millions of people

ordered them.

Jessica Peach invented a toy when she was only eight. She liked to

jump rope. When you jump alone, you need a short rope. With friends,

you need a long rope. So Jessica invented an _____

jump rope. It can be long or short. When you aren't jumping, it can turn

into a belt!

Word List

adjustable
business
company
created
recycled

Think About It!

How is Jessica's invention different from a regular jump rope?

Name _____ Date _____

How Leopard Got His Spots

Did you ever wonder how leopards got their spots? Fill in the blanks in this tale that tells the story.

One African _____ tells how Leopard got his spots. Leopard and some other animals had a funeral march for their friend Ant. As the animals walked, Leopard's stomach _____. He was hungry!

Passing a farm, Leopard noticed some baskets filled with fresh eggs. First, he tossed one egg into his mouth. Soon, he had eaten an _____ basket! The farmer saw the empty basket. "Who stole my eggs?" he asked. They all denied it.

The farmer had an idea. He asked all the animals to jump over a _____. He said the animal who had eaten the eggs would fall in. Each animal _____ over the flames. When it was Leopard's turn, he took a deep breath, jumped, and landed in the fire. "Aha!" said the farmer. "It was you!" Leopard climbed out of the fire, but his coat was _____ in spots as a reminder of his greed.

Word List

- bonfire
- entire
- folktale
- leaped
- rumbled
- scorched

Think About It!

What happened after the farmer saw the empty basket?

Quick Cloze Passages for Boosting Comprehension: Grades 2–3 © 2012 by Scholastic Teaching Resources

Name _____ Date _____

Vanishing Frogs

It's fun to try to find frogs in the woods and near rivers.
But in some cases, that's harder and harder to do.
Fill in the blanks to find out why frogs are vanishing.

Frogs have lived on this planet for millions of

years. But recently, _____

have noticed that certain types of frogs are

_____. Some species have even

become _____. What's the problem?

Experts have two theories:

Word List

chemicals
destroyed
disappearing
extinct
scientists

● **Ruined homes:** Many frogs live in ponds or other wet areas.

People have dried up these areas in order to build roads or

buildings. Some other frogs live in forests. Many forests have been

_____ so that people can use the land.

That leaves fewer places for frogs to live.

● **Pollution:** _____ get into the ponds and

lands where many frogs live. Some experts say this pollution

makes frogs sick.

Think About It!

What might be done to help protect frogs?

Quick Close Passages for Boosting Comprehension: Grades 2–3 © 2012 by Scholastic Teaching Resources

Name _____ Date _____

The Best Sand Castle

What would you see at a sand castle contest? Fill in the blanks in this article to find out.

It is 37 feet high. It weighs 19,000 tons. It is as long as a

_____ field. It has roads so that you can

walk through it. Believe it or not—it's a sand castle

in Florida!

Many beach towns around the world have sand castle

contests. Some people build other _____

things, such as sand sculptures of animals, food, and people. Some

builders enter the contests to win the _____,

and others enter just for fun.

South Padre Island, Texas, has a sand castle contest every year.

The builders find their own spaces to build on the beach. For two days,

they use sand and water to _____ different shapes.

Then the _____ choose the best sand sculptures.

There is a special contest for kids. They make crazy sand animals,

and other very silly sculptures. People who are watching vote for the

best ones.

Word List

- football
- interesting
- judges
- mold
- prizes

Think About It!

What kinds of sculptures do people make at sand castle contests?

Quick Cloze Passages for Boosting Comprehension: Grades 2–3 © 2012 by Scholastic Teaching Resources

Name _____ Date _____

The Story of Ping Pong

How is Ping Pong related to tennis? Read this article to find out. Use the word list to fill in the missing words.

Ping pong is the sound of a small _____ ball being batted across a net. It's also the name of the game. The formal name for ping pong is "table tennis." In fact, ping pong is quite a bit like tennis—except for the table. Which came first? Tennis did.

Kings played tennis more than 500 years ago. They played on stone floors in huge rooms inside _____.

In 1874, tennis moved outdoors. A brilliant man named Walter Wingfield drew up plans for a new kind of "lawn tennis" court. He also changed some of the rules.

Table tennis, or ping pong, is a _____ version of tennis. The ball and paddle are smaller than tennis balls and _____. It was first played in the 1880s.

The _____ of a small-scale tennis court was drawn on top of the table, and a net placed across the center.

Think About It!

In what ways are tennis and ping pong alike and different?

Quick Cloze Passages for Boosting Comprehension: Grades 2–3 © 2012 by Scholastic Teaching Resources

Name _____ Date _____

America's Lady Liberty

Who is America's Lady Liberty? Why is she important to our nation? Fill in the blanks in this article to find out.

She stands in New York Harbor, _____ and tall. She is a breathtaking sight with her majestic crown and her blazing torch held high.

For more than 100 years, day and night, this wonderful lady has _____ visitors to our shores. She has never tired of her job. Nor has she ever _____ to thrill those who see her for the first time. To all Americans and to all who come to America from afar, she stands as a symbol of _____.

Who is this great lady? Some people call her Lady Liberty. You may know her as the Statue of Liberty. She was a gift from France for America's 100th birthday. She was _____ here in 350 pieces. Putting the statue together took four months.

Word List

failed
freedom
greeted
proud
shipped

Think About It!

Find one fact and one opinion in the article above.

Quick Cloze Passages for Boosting Comprehension: Grades 2–3 © 2012 by Scholastic Teaching Resources

Name _____ Date _____

Life in Space

What would it be like to live in space? Fill in the blanks from the word list as you read about some of the things that affect life in space.

When astronauts go to work in space, they are too far away to _____ home each night. They have to live in space for a short time to do their work. But life in space is different from life on earth! The main reason is that there is less gravity. Gravity is the _____ force that holds everything— even you—to the earth. With less gravity, astronauts' feet don't stay on the ground, so they float instead of walk. It feels a bit like _____. At night, astronauts sleep in sleeping bags strapped to the walls so they don't float around. To eat without pots and pans flying, astronauts have special food like freeze-dried _____ eggs. To get clean, astronauts rub soap and water on their bodies and _____ it off. That's because a shower would spray all over.

Word List

commute
invisible
scrambled
sponge
swimming

Think About It! What effect does less gravity have on astronauts working in space?

Quick Cloze Passages for Boosting Comprehension: Grades 2–3 © 2012 by Scholastic Teaching Resources

Name _____ Date _____

Leonardo Da Vinci

Read this article to learn about some of the amazing things created by Leonardo da Vinci. Use the word list to fill in the missing words.

Leonardo da Vinci was born in Italy over 500 years ago. He had many talents and ideas. He was a true

_____.

Leonardo was an _____. He drew a picture of a bicycle. At the time, that was a new idea. The first bicycle was built 300 years later. He also drew a picture of an airplane, another new idea. The first airplane was built 400 years later. Leonardo never ran out of ideas.

Leonardo was also a great painter. He painted the *Mona Lisa.* The woman in the painting has a _____ look on her face. What is she thinking? Why is she smiling? As you walk in front of the painting, her eyes seem to follow you.

Leonardo _____ nature and asked questions. Why do waves form in water? Why does the moon shine? He wrote his ideas in a notebook... backwards! Today, people use a _____ to read his notes!

Think About It! .... What were some of Leonardo da Vinci's accomplishments?

Quick Cloze Passages for Boosting Comprehension: Grades 2–3 © 2012 by Scholastic Teaching Resources

An American Volcano

What do you know about volcanoes? Fill in the blanks in this article to find out more about one in our country.

Mount Saint Helens is an active volcano in the state of Washington. In 1980, this volcano erupted, spewing hot _____ into the air. Explosions caused a huge cloud of dust. This gray dust filled the air and settled on houses and cars many miles away. The thick dust made it hard for people and animals to _____. The explosions _____ trees on the side of the mountain. The hot rocks _____ forest fires. The snow that was on the mountain melted quickly, causing _____ and mud slides. Mount Saint Helens still erupts from time to time, but not as badly as it did in 1980. But who knows when it will blow its top again!

Word List

breathe
flattened
floods
ignited
lava

Think About It!

What effect did the dust from Mt. Saint Helens have on the area around it?

Name _____ Date _____

Titanic!

Why is the _Titanic_ such a famous ship?
Fill in the blanks in this article to find out.

People said it was the safest ship ever built. It was the largest, for sure. They called it a "floating _____." It had a big gym, tennis courts, and a huge swimming pool. There were _____ dining rooms and ballrooms.

It set sail for New York in 1912 with 2,000 people on board. There were over 40 tons of potatoes and over 6,000 pounds of butter. There were more than two tons of coffee to drink.

Not long into the trip, the _Titanic_ struck an _____. The "safest ship" began to sink. There were not enough _____. The ship and most of its passengers sank to the bottom of the sea. About 1,500 people died that night.

In 1986, the wreck of the _Titanic_ was found. Divers removed and brought up more than 5,000 _____. These included jewelry, coins, postcards, and magazines. What was believed to be the safest ship is now famous for a very sad ending.

Word List

- artifacts
- elegant
- iceberg
- lifeboats
- palace

Think About It!

What caused the _Titanic_ to sink?

Name _____   Date _____

Jackie Robinson: American Hero

Who was Jackie Robinson? Why is he an American hero? Fill in the blanks in this biography to find out.

There was a time in the United Sates when African Americans could not go to the same schools as white people. They could not drink from the same water _____. They were also not allowed to play major league baseball.

Word List

- brave
- chances
- fountains
- owner
- warned

Two special men changed that. One was an African-American baseball player named Jackie Robinson. The other was a white baseball club _____ named Branch Rickey. Together, these two men worked to make sure African Americans had the same _____ as others to play baseball.

In 1947, Branch Rickey asked Jackie to play for the Brooklyn Dodgers. He _____ Jackie that he might face some angry fans and players. Jackie was _____ and kept his cool. In his first year, he was named Rookie of the Year. Today, he's in the Hall of Fame.

Think About It!   How would you describe Jackie Robinson and Branch Rickey?

Three Cheers for Chocolate

Who doesn't like chocolate?! Fill in the blanks in this article to read more about everyone's favorite treat.

How do you like to eat chocolate? Do you munch on candy bars? Do you put _____ on ice cream? Do you drink it? Any way you have it, chocolate is _____!

The first chocolate was made in Central America. People there drank it about a thousand years ago. It was cold and bitter, not _____. But one king drank 50 cups a day.

In 1528, Spanish _____ brought chocolate to Spain. The Spanish added _____ and vanilla. Then someone _____ it and made hot chocolate! By the mid 1600s, rich people all over Europe drank hot chocolate. In the 1700s, people brought chocolate to North America. In the 1800s, people made the first chocolate bars.

Today, there are cookbooks, Web sites, and clubs just for chocolate lovers. It's hard to imagine a world without chocolate!

Word List

- delicious
- explorers
- heated
- sprinkles
- sugar
- sweet

Think About It!

Name one fact and one opinion in this article.

Quick Cloze Passages for Boosting Comprehension: Grades 2–3 © 2012 by Scholastic Teaching Resources

Name _____ Date _____

Vets Behind the Scenes

What do you do if your pet is sick? Read this article to find out who can help. Use the word list to fill in the missing words.

What happens when a hippo gets a runny nose? Who aids a shark when it has a toothache? Zoos and aquariums have vets on hand to make sure their patients stay healthy and happy.

Dr. Peregrine Wolff is a vet at Disney's Animal Kingdom. She cares for more than 1,000 _____. She takes special care of new arrivals. "They are like kids going to camp," she says. They're making new friends, eating new food, and learning new _____." She keeps the new "campers" away from others at first, to make sure they aren't sick.

When Inky the whale arrived at the National Aquarium in Baltimore, Maryland, she had lost her _____. The vets there noticed she wasn't eating, so they gave her a series of tests. They found the problem in her belly—ocean _____, like plastic bags and wrappers. That kind of _____ would spoil anybody's first day at camp!

Think About It!

What are some things a vet does at a zoo or aquarium?

Answer Key

These word lists show the correct order of the words that complete each cloze passage.

Passage 1: guess, mittens, shovel, wiggle, nodded

Passage 2: history, special, salute, praise, proudly

Passage 3: ahead, slipped, rut, splash, mighty

Passage 4: freezing, gusts, drifts, uncover, swirling

Passage 5: drenched, meanings, sense, pouring, ruined

Passage 6: communicate, attention, greeting, different, stretches

Passage 7: huge, flowed, ceiling, underwater, floating

Passage 8: beautiful, load, permission, lowered, froze

Passage 9: waiting, video, married, comb, cavity, surprise

Passage 10: invented, watched, tumbled, amusing, machine

Passage 11: study, camera, finally, photographs, wonderful

Passage 12: beneath, terrified, thundering, solid, laughed

Passage 13: competing, type, weave, tunnels, scored, performing

Passage 14: troops, filthy, sweat, outraged, uniform

Passage 15: giant, millions, helium, volunteers, directors

Passage 16: weapon, returns, airplane, shoulder, exactly

Passage 17: amazing, underground, chambers, repaired, system, dynamite

Passage 18: several, cafeteria, remembers, favorite, embarrassed

Passage 19: thousands, munch, seafood, flippers, hatch

Passage 20: squirm, dislike, practice, science, control

Passage 21: gadgets, adult, construct, clothespin, mobiles

Passage 22: supposed, rude, stab, afford, strict

Passage 23: tracks, thawed, terrible, mosquitoes, drill

Passage 24: enemies, secure, connected, extended, symbol

Passage 25: telephone, buddies, sprang, backyard, naughty

Passage 26: continents, desert, powerful, pouches, webbed

Passage 27: darted, classrooms, human, squeezes, reward

Passage 28: business, created, recycled, company, adjustable

Passage 29: folktale, rumbled, entire, bonfire, leaped, scorched

Passage 30: scientists, disappearing, extinct, destroyed, chemicals

Passage 31: football, interesting, prizes, mold, judges

Passage 32: plastic, castles, miniature, racquets, outline

Passage 33: proud, greeted, failed, freedom, shipped

Passage 34: commute, invisible, swimming, scrambled, sponge

Passage 35: genius, inventor, puzzled, studied, mirror

Passage 36: lava, breathe, flattened, ignited, floods

Passage 37: palace, elegant, iceberg, lifeboats, artifacts

Passage 38: fountains, owner, chances, warned, brave

Passage 39: sprinkles, delicious, sweet, explorers, sugar, heated

Passage 40: creatures, activities, appetite, litter, stomachache